Surviving Sports and the Game of Life

Your Holistic Guide to Achieving World-Class Results

Surviving Sports and the Game of Life

Your Holistic Guide to Achieving World-Class Results

By Frederick Entenmann

ISBN: 978-1-945446-00-9

YouSpeakIt
P U B L I S H I N G
The Easy Way
to Get Your Book
Done Right™

www.YouSpeakItPublishing.com

Dedication

To those who lack an encouraging leader or positive mentor in their lives.

To anyone who carries emotional trauma, negative experiences, or scars associated with an abusive bully, scathing coach, unsupportive parent, nay-saying friend, berating mentor, or negative teacher.

To Fred Entenmann, the young, bright boy who held on to his heart, intuition, and vivid visions and never stopped dreaming big.

Acknowledgments

I want to thank the following individuals from the depths of my heart:

My parents, family members, and friends (you know who you are) whose unconditional contributions of love and support helped me through extremely challenging phases of my life.

Kim, you are a world-class healer, an empath, a bright spirit, and a light of profound beauty whose rare emotional intelligence and compassionate heart helped me heal deep-rooted traumas, and to expand, let go and reconnect me with my authentic soul.

John Assaraf, for your top-notch mentoring, guidance, support, and infinite positivity.

My children, Magnus and Lilian, you are blessed, treasured souls who light up the universe and have made all the difference in my world. I am truly blessed.

Keith and Maura Leon, for giving me an opportunity and taking me on this journey. I appreciate your professionalism, authentic heart-centeredness, support, and words of wisdom. Keith, you are my soul brother. Thanks for cracking my heart wide open.

Steven E Schmitt, for your open arms and sound advice any minute of the day, for your love and positive support for my first book. You rock, brother. Your heart is huge.

Table of Contents

Introduction

Whether you are an amateur or professional in the sports world, an adult, teen, or child, this book is your fundamental guide on how to achieve lasting real-life success. Whether you have already achieved your target level in sports or you want to break through plateaus and achieve new heights in performance, this book is a holistic guide to achieving world-class results.

Inside you will find comprehensive resources that will help you attain more:

- Confidence
- Mental clarity
- Focus
- Centeredness
- Balance and alignment
- Joy
- Health
- Wellness

This is a manual that will offer you life-skills that will prepare you:

- To become the kind of person you know you can be

- To set yourself up for authentic soul success

- To lead the kind of life you know you deserve

- To bring you the confidence, security, happiness, fulfillment, and ultimate vitality that everybody wants

There is no secret to achieving life fulfillment. Your life starts with *you*. It goes above and beyond wishing.

It requires planning and implementing with the right resources.

It involves:

- Trusting
- Letting go
- Tapping into your inner knowing heart
- Letting your intuitive self flow outward accordingly

There is only one you. You are greatness.

CHAPTER ONE

Mind

FOCUS

Focus is absolutely essential. When you enter any sphere of endeavor, it is the one preliminary necessity. An athlete may commit countless hours to training, but without focus, it won't be possible to convert those efforts into results.

I think it is safe to say that all athletes want to reach their full potential. Focus is what separates an average performance from a great performance.

An unfocused mind will deliver a jumbled performance. It is no coincidence that the athletes that we most admire are the most focused. Focus enables an athlete to perform effectively amidst countless distractions and diversions.

In order to attain a laser-like focus, you must be 110 percent committed to whatever you are doing. Commitment means having an ultra-specific goal or vision and doing whatever is necessary to reach it.

The focus that top achievers are able to attain is not out of the ordinary. It's simply a lost art. And that is why I am presenting this information to you; it is a guide to the art of reaching your focused potential. Followed properly, it will enable you to become your own master and realize your full potential.

Focus on Your Outcomes — What Do You Want?

Many athletes I know are focused on the wrong outcomes. People often get preoccupied with messages they are receiving from others, and so the outcomes they emphasize in practice are ego-centrically misaligned. Think carefully about the outcomes you seek.

What do *you* want?

The only way you are going to get the outcome you seek is by connecting with yourself and using yourself as an expression through the sport. This explains why extremely focused athletes like Steffi Graf, Michael Jordan, Jerry Rice, Roger Federer, and Wayne Gretzky offer a rare creativity to their game. They achieve a laser focus that is in complete alignment with themselves, regardless of the circumstances. For them, the sport becomes an expressive art form; they are composers, comfortable with focusing on themselves, and their unique artistry comes out beautifully through their game.

The problem arises when individuals get preoccupied with circumstances outside of themselves and focus becomes completely misaligned — what I call *shattered*. A shattered athlete is unfocused, mentally and emotionally. Poor decision-making usually follows. They may end up with such a total misalignment of the mind that expression and outcome become undesirable no matter how many times it may be rehearsed. Eventually, it leads to the meltdown of athletes.

Elite athletes are very specific about the outcomes they seek. It is what separates amateur from professional. They know exactly what they would like to achieve and disregard anything but that. This means that distractions and negativity don't even come within the realm of their focus. Their boundaries are so strongly rooted that under no circumstance do they allow others to influence the outcome. You can learn a great deal by observing athletes like this.

Focus and Performance

The more you can achieve focus, the better chance you will have to achieve what you are seeking through your sport, through your body. The outcome of your performance is directly proportional to your focus.

Focus is also a type of programming to your mind.

For instance, an athlete can purposely direct their focus to the specific outcome that they desire:

- A basket in basketball
- A goal in soccer
- A touchdown in football
- Pitching a perfect game in baseball

The more you focus on that specific outcome, the more precise it becomes, and your brain will know nothing other than achieving that outcome. As a result, thought turns into vivid picture, a visualization, and before you know it, you are turning your rehearsed thinking into doing. That is the definition of directed focus. One way to do this is to write down your goals and reflect on them often.

Focus on the *Now*

Focusing on the *now* is probably the most important component of the entire focus sphere. What happened yesterday is gone, and what happens in the future will be mandated by your present focus. This means that whatever you are focusing on is going to become a manifestation of what you are thinking. So by staying in the *now*, you will appreciate fully the outcome that you wish to receive in the future.

This is a very important lesson and so important to practice as a dedicated athlete that I wish someone had told me about it in my formative years. It is a skill that takes countless hours of concentrated practice to develop. With all of the distractions in the modern world, focusing as an athlete has never been more difficult.

To bring your focus to the *now*:

- Constantly write down your goals.
- Review what it is you want to achieve.
- Record what you wish to represent.
- Record who you wish to be.

Keeping your focus in the present and forgetting the past is difficult, but it is necessary. Whatever you focus on in the *now* will be realized in the future.

Focus is the culmination of your thoughts and attention. Be wary of distractions. If you are not 100 percent committed to your outcomes, your focus will waver. It is gaining consistent awareness and attentiveness to the outcome that will sharpen your focus. Laser focus equals massive results.

PRESENCE

Have you noticed that there are athletes who are leading performers in their sport, but are utter disasters in real life?

This issue is a conundrum in the modern sports world.

How can high-achieving athletes have such a lack of presence in life?

Presence is awareness of your immediate environment, both external and internal. Lack of this awareness can have a negative effect on playing field performance, but it also impacts performance in athletes' personal lives.

Personally, when I was a professional, Division-I athlete, I let opinions, judgments, and distractions from media, coaches, and teammates affect my presence and this deeply impacted my personal relationships.

To learn the art of presence takes practice. Just like the many hours it takes to acquire any sports skill, it requires effort to attain presence in life.

Distractions

When you become successful in the sports world, you will quickly be asked to shoulder a large number of new responsibilities. The number of distractions are immeasurable, especially with respect to the media. With the advent of online media and social networking, information comes to us at a remarkable rate and the pressure to keep up is intense.

An athlete experiences a constant barrage of stimuli that can be overwhelming. You will need to learn how to ignore the hype and guard your energy. It is vital to protect yourself from external noise that only diverts energy from your efforts to focus. Ultimately, it will negatively affect your progress.

Only a clear, focused mind is going to lead to your best performance. Needless distractions don't move you closer to your goals; the more you can identify and eliminate them, the more focused and energized you will be.

In order to protect yourself:

- Sit down and make a list of everything in your life that is a distraction. I urge you to eliminate these things.

- Practice this daily and write everything in a journal.

- Make a timeline of what you are eliminating and when. Make this a priority and focus primarily on the outcomes you want; never on what you *don't* want.

- Start a morning and evening ritual during which you review your goals in your journal.

Negativity

Negativity has to be the biggest cancer in the sports world.

You may experience negativity coming from many sources:

- Media
- Coaches
- Teammates

It is a low vibrating dark energy that can do immeasurable harm to an athlete. Words carry a vibration that resonates with your very cells and sends a ripple of current that spreads across and around the entire planet. The vibration sends a signal to your brain, where it can cause harmful changes.

It is scientifically proven that negative words can be stored as trauma within our cells. The outcome can be mentally, physically, and perpetually damaging.

Many athletes don't possess the proper skills to process negativity and respond to it in a healthy way. In the competitive world we are often taught not to speak up at all when we are mistreated. Setting personal boundaries with coaches, teammates, and the press is very difficult.

As a young man, I didn't protect myself very well. I

responded to negativity by internalizing my emotions. Eventually, my inability to handle all of the criticism, derision, shame, and guilt resulted in the onset of post-traumatic stress disorder (PTSD).

I am now on a mission to educate athletes about healthy responses to negativity. Always be the master of yourself and speak your truth! An athlete's life is one of high pressure and stress; we are always asking ourselves to move faster and try harder. Athletes need to be taught how to slow down enough to emotionally process everything coming at them and learn to advocate for themselves when things are not going well.

How important is fighting negativity?

The legendary and beloved John Wooden, who led his UCLA team to a remarkable ten NCAA Men's Basketball Championships, strongly believed in guarding against negativity. He didn't even believe in cursing because he knew that a single word could be a negative and damaging signal to the brain. Negativity destroys human potential and thus, any hope of achieving positive results.

Think about it: what do you want to be as an athlete? Don't you want to reach your highest potential, to have unwavering confidence? Negativity shouldn't even enter your domain if you are seeking to break through plateaus and attain the next level.

To fight negativity:

- Surround yourself with positivity as much as possible.

- Set personal boundaries and speak up when your boundaries are violated.

- Keep your thoughts positive and take care to be a positive influence on others.

- Be the inspiring light that helps lift your teammates to greatness.

Meditation

If I could choose just one tool to give athletes to help their performance and quality of life, it would be meditation. It is my number one go-to strategy.

Meditation can improve so many areas that are important to athletes:

- Thinking
- Focus
- Outlook
- Awareness
- Intuition
- Connection

There are a lot of misconceptions and misinformation

about meditation; it is often seen as a kind of hocus-pocus or a mysterious religious practice. Meditation is simply quieting the mind.

In that quiet space you can focus inward on yourself and simply *be* in the moment:

- Focus on this thought: *Be here now.*
- Slow down
- Quiet your mind
- Breathe

It is simple but incredibly powerful.

I once heard John Salley (four-time NBA champion) talking about former Chicago Bulls coach Phil Jackson in an interview with Rich Roll. Salley said that the most essential component of his team coming together was Coach Phil's use of meditation in the locker room. There is absolutely nothing more beneficial to your team than helping the players share meditative thought patterns. Coach Phil, called *The Zen Master* by his players because of his use of Zen-Buddhist techniques, was also able to calmly and artfully manage many intense personalities, including Dennis Rodman, and brought his teams to eleven NBA championships.

During meditation, anxiety diminishes, overthinking ceases, and the negativity associated with anything external (family issues, personal problems) fades away.

A quiet mind enables you to find inner comfort, poise, and concentration.

Tapping into these internal resources gives an athlete a great advantage in competition but can also be helpful when meeting any of life's challenges. Slow down and breathe.

Empirical research continues to expose the countless benefits of meditation. Meditation not only increases IQ through stimulating neurons and creating new neural pathways in the brain, but it also is very healing for anything traumatic or stressful. One study in particular from Harvard found, after subjects meditated, there was increased gray-matter density in the hippocampus, known to be important for learning and memory, and in structures associated with self-awareness, compassion, and introspection. Participant-reported reductions in stress also were correlated with decreased gray-matter density in the amygdala, which is known to play an important role in anxiety and stress.

Meditation, when done properly, can be a highly effective method of dopamine increase. Dopamine is a neurotransmitter that helps control the brain's reward and pleasure centers and also helps regulate movement and emotional response. It enables us not only to see rewards, but also to take action to move toward them.

Have you ever been in a conversation with someone, and their mouth is moving, but their body language lets you know that their mind is somewhere else?

Distractibility and overthinking are very common and are particularly damaging to an athlete's concentration. Overthinking can become a compulsion that leaves us in a perplexed state and can have a negative effect on personal development. These issues impacted me tremendously and I had to learn to change my thinking patterns. Meditation was the key.

When I added meditation to my daily rituals, it changed my life profoundly.

I noticed improvement in many areas:

- Clarity of thought
- Reactions to stress
- Ability to calm myself in stressful situations
- Constructive response to criticism

I was able to tap into valuable resources that I hadn't ever known were even there. When you are able to tap into these internal resources, your potential as an athlete will go up exponentially and your performance will reach new heights.

The more awareness we gain of ourselves, the more awareness we gain of our surroundings, and that awareness can improve performance in any sport.

When your mind is at ease, you will be able to reach the athletic flow state much more easily.

You will find that meditation clears out the mental clutter and replaces it with more useful feelings and thoughts:

- Connection
- Presence
- Gratitude for just being alive

We are finally catching up to what Buddhist monks — who can live well beyond 100 years and lead the most peaceful lives known — have been aware of for thousands of years: Meditation and mindfulness are essential to a healthy mind. These practices enable you to connect with yourself and your environment, and naturally lead to rewards on the field and in life.

Learning how to achieve a quiet mind produces outcomes such as:

- Ease
- Joy
- Lightness
- Success

These outcomes will flow to you and your friends, family, teammates, and other relationships as well.

CREATIVENESS AND VISUALIZATION

Creativeness and visualization are important concepts in sports, and are commonly misunderstood.

As a twelve-year-old, I became intrigued by the idea of visualization when I read about how Larry Bird used the technique before games and also in the pre-season. Larry Bird was a three-time NBA champion with the Celtics and also a three-time NBA MVP. Often criticized for being nonathletic, he obviously had other vital skills. Although he wasn't a natural athlete, he was an extraordinary player, mentally tough and able to perform under pressure. He understood the power of his mind and how he could use it in the athletic realm.

So what is visualization?

Visualization is simply creating the outcome that you wish to play out. It requires the creative part of your mind and uses pictures, images, and words assembled on what I envision as a big screen.

When you visualize, you *create* what you would like to see in your future and put it on your canvas; you can invent the playing field scenario before you even get there. You are so much more powerful than you know. We have the power as human beings to get outside our physical bodies and actually create whatever it is we want to achieve.

This is yet another essential life skill that needs to be practiced, something to work on regularly.

Every morning upon waking and every evening before you sleep:

- Visualize the life that you want.

- Incorporate all your senses (sight, sound, taste, feel, touch) into your vision.

- Jump into this scenario and feel it as if you already have it.

Remember, if you can see it, you can believe it.

Manifesting

Manifesting is another misunderstood concept. It comes across as very metaphysical, which it is, but it is actually as easy as making a free throw is for a seasoned basketball player. Manifesting is bringing what you visualize into being. I've known a lot of people who can do this without thinking about it.

Have you ever met one of these people?

They set out to achieve something and it all seems to come so easily.

How do they do it?

It's all about visualization. These individuals know exactly what they want, they picture it in their minds, and involve all their senses until it becomes an integral part of their being. It is transformed from a *visualization* into an *experience*; this is manifesting. They tell the story they want and BOOM! They create it; before you know it, the physical manifestation of what they want appears. I can't tell you how many times I have manifested things in my life. You also have the power!

This is a skill. You have to create powerful visualizations in order to manifest what you want. For instance, I was able to manifest my soul-life partner when I was able to visualize exactly who I wanted. You can manifest a home, a desired dream job, or anything else you can visualize. There are no limits when it comes to manifestation. We are not taught in school that we have the power to create or manifest. There is no educational degree required. You are equipped with all you need.

Go for it!

Remember, you just have to know exactly what you want and live it as if it is already there. Be creative! It is important to mention that this process can't be forced; it is common for people immersed in the discipline of sports to turn to the use of militant techniques. Manifestation, however, requires unresisting flow. This is why children grow in leaps and bounds overnight. The less you try, the more you are going to manifest. That is the ultimate secret. Just let it flow.

Your Unique You

It seems like we have been forever told how to act, how to play, what to believe, what is cool and what is not. But remember this; we were all born onto this Earth with our own distinctive fingerprints, as unique, real, live, thinking, feeling human beings. Think about that. There is no other human being in the entire world exactly like you. This suggests to me that our souls are the same way: unique.

If you want to be a top-tier athlete or evolve in any way in your life, you will have to question your own personal belief system. Most notably, this requires developing an appreciation of your unique self; it requires self-love. Only *you* know what you have to offer, who you are, what you stand for, and how you want to be.

To start, work on your personal belief system in your journal:

- Write down five things you think you stand for.

- Add anything additional that you want to stand for.

- Reflect on this list daily as a testimony for who you are.

- Under no circumstance should you let any coach, teammate, form of media, or other external force change your list.

Stand strong and always stay true to yourself.

Acknowledgment of your unique self requires a sense of awareness and self-love and at its extreme, the willingness to die for what you stand for.

Have you ever noticed that our society is mesmerized by this kind of greatness?

Muhammad Ali, for example, was blatantly and boldly truthful to his very soul. The media knew they would never get anything from him other than the real Muhammad Ali and what he stood for.

Not only did Muhammad Ali excel in his sport, he also transcended the sport beyond all levels by becoming a worldwide ambassador for peace. You will see that when you stand strong as *you*, people will respect you and they won't be able to wait to hear what you have to say.

We as a society admire the bold truth, and you are only going to speak your truth when you appreciate and love the unique being that you are. So stay true to yourself.

When you are part of a team, you will have a unique role in that team framework, but you do not have to change who you are in order to fit that role. In fact, if you are in tune with who you are, you will naturally be comfortable with being in that role. There is much more to progressing in sports than becoming a rich and famous star. Just honor yourself and recognize that your unique you is your own personal expression, so love yourself and let that come out.

Your Natural Genius

Plato, one of history's greatest philosophers, stated that he truly believed we are all born onto this Earth with the answers; the truth resides within our souls. Each and every one of us has a unique genius. We all have something to offer.

Once you realize this, those ten thousand pounds of pressure you may feel like you are wearing on your shoulders will just float away effortlessly. Realize just how special and unique a genius you are. It is so easy to get caught up in the competition in a sport, which only brings comparison and intensity and things that don't matter.

Don't ever forget the uniqueness that you have to offer and the genius that resides within you. In the long term, the most devastating, degrading thing you can do is compare yourself to other people. Just realize your unique gifts are yours to offer to the world and you just need to tap in and let your light shine brightly. There are no limits!

The highest quality coaches will respect your uniqueness and provide you with support and guidance. Controlling and manipulating and telling you that you are not worthy or good enough are not examples of good coaching. I urge those athletes that might be in an abusive coaching situation to walk away and seek the atmosphere or situation that you know you deserve.

There are many techniques and practices you can use to learn to respect and expand upon your natural genius. While the list is endless, it starts by practicing just one: visualization. If I can offer any form of beneficial advice, it would be to use that big screen. Our minds are powerful, and dreaming big goes a long way.

The universe wants us to succeed; it wants us to realize our goals and be creative geniuses. We have the power and capability to create whatever we want. Quoting the late Coach Jimmy Valvano: "Don't ever give up!" Stop creating limits, they are merely self-imposed ego trips that only hold you back.

The more we practice the skill of visualizing and using our creativity, the better we're going to be as athletes and human beings. We will be able to expand and push the brink of our potential, like the greatest athletes in sports, but also like Einstein, DaVinci, and Edison, as well as more recent examples of genius like Mark Zuckerberg, Steve Jobs, Elon Musk, Oprah Winfrey and Richard Branson.

CHAPTER TWO

Nutrition and Recovery

PAIN AND INFLAMMATION

Pain and inflammation are common chronic symptoms among athletes, as well as the general public. In mild form they can sap energy and reduce performance; when severe, they can be completely incapacitating. There is nothing more debilitating to an athletic career than pain and inflammation.

I have seen first-hand that if you take the preventative and nutritional approaches to eliminate, or at least reduce them, your quality of life will become exponentially better. Taking the appropriate steps to free yourself from pain and inflammation takes knowledge and effort, but it will be worthwhile.

The cause of exercise-induced inflammation is microscopic damage to your tissues during training. Inflammation is an immune system response to tissue damage. Its function is to remove cellular debris from the site of damage and initiate repair. When muscles are inflamed, they are typically sore and also lose strength, endurance and range of motion.

The key elements in addressing these problems are:

- Body chemistry
- Hydration
- Nutrition

Alkalization

Alkalization is the new buzzword in the performance industry.

What is it exactly?

Like the planet on which you live, your body is 70 percent water. Your brain is 83 percent water and your muscles are 75 percent water. And like the oceans, the pH of your body's sea is critical. Your blood has to maintain a pH of 7.365. If that pH is only slightly altered to just 7.0, which is more acidic, you would die from poisoning by your own blood. The more acidic your body is the less energy you will have. It causes aches and stiffness. It affects all levels of performance on a cellular level. So what this means, without getting too technical, is that raising your body pH level from acidic to alkaline may help to reduce some symptoms of inflammation and pain.

Some symptoms of acidosis are:

- Chronic muscle pain or cramps
- Constant fatigue
- Easily running out of breath
- Feeling like you can't get enough air

A saliva pH test may be helpful. When your pH level falls, your body attempts to regulate itself in a natural way by capturing and storing some excessively acidic substances in organs such as your kidneys, liver and lungs, thereby maintaining optimal blood pH. These acidic substances ultimately begin to attack your healthy cells, causing them to be toxic, damaged and sick. In time, if the issue isn't addressed these cells can grow uncontrollably and spread to other parts or organs in your body.

Some of the reasons for chronic acidosis in the twenty-first century are:

- A diet high in meat, sugar, and highly processed food

- Overconsumption of caffeine and alcohol

- Pesticides, additives, and growth hormones used to make and grow our food

One of the best ways to combat acidosis is to flush the body with alkaline water.

Additionally you can eat alkaline rich foods, such as:

- Kale
- Cucumber
- Celery
- Spinach
- Avocado
- Broccoli
- Bell peppers

For the most benefit, eat them raw.

Not all water is created equal. You are what you consume. If you drink acidic water, you're going to be acidic. Most sodas and carbonated drinks are around pH 4.0. This is acidic. If you drink alkaline, ionized water, your body will be alkaline. The pH of most purified and distilled water is around 5.0–6.0. If your cells don't get the buffering they need from the water you provide them, they are going to pull alkalizing mineral salts from the bones, muscles, and elsewhere in the body. Those areas will be more vulnerable to pain, inflammation, disease, and low performance.

Disease is less likely to thrive in an alkaline environment. Cancer and other debilitating, life-threatening diseases thrive in an acidic state. The sooner you practice keeping your body in an alkalized environment, the healthier and more vital you will be.

Alkaline water is extremely powerful. It assists your body in balancing pH by eliminating strong acidic residue and does so without damaging healthy cells. An alkaline diet is also high in hydrogen, now scientifically proven to be a significant holistic healing component.

If you support your body with an alkaline diet:

- You will have more energy and feel less sluggish.

- Soreness and inflammation will be reduced.

- You will be less susceptible to cramping, fatigue, and injury.

- Muscles will operate and recover better and athletic performance will improve.

- You will be more resistant to disease.

If you don't have access to water that promotes alkalization, you can make it yourself from the recipe below.

Ingredients:

1 teaspoon Himalayan salt
2 liters of clean, filtered water
A few slices of an organic lemon

How to Prepare:

1. Fill a jar with 2 liters of water.

2. Add the lemon slices. Make sure you don't squeeze the lemon.

3. Add the teaspoon of Himalayan salt, cover the jar and let it stay overnight at room temperature.

4. In the morning, before eating or drinking anything else, drink three 6 ounce glasses of the water.

This drink will help you achieve the perfect alkaline balance in the body. Your body will be grateful and you will appreciate your new performance and recovery levels!

Hydration and the Sports Drink Dilemma

It is clear that good hydration is vital to preventing and healing inflammation.

We've already discussed the benefits of alkalizing water, but what about all the specialized sports drinks that are available?

There has always been a great deal of hype about sports drinks and it can be difficult to figure out what is true and what is not. In recent years the advertising has focused on condemning fast-acting sugars, claiming that these substances cause an energy spike followed by an energy crash that wreaks havoc on performance.

According to this viewpoint, slower-acting sugars and non-sugar carbohydrates are better, because they provide a steady supply of energy that does not terminate in a crash. Be cautious about any claims from advertisements. All of these companies have their own motives.

What would the sports world do without the billions injected into sponsorship by corporations like McDonalds, Coca-Cola, or Red Bull?

Yes, sports drinks can hydrate you, provide electrolytes, and even help you make the most of your exercise. But it is deception: they're not miracle drinks, and they aren't necessarily even better than water — especially when it comes to hydration.

Unless you're a professional athlete or an iron man contender, you don't need the electrolytes or calories from sports drinks during your daily routine.

If you work out for half-an-hour and then drink three Gatorades, you're consuming far more calories than you have burned during your workout — if your goal is weight loss, you aren't going to help yourself at all. A typical 20-ounce bottle has 130 calories and 34 grams of refined sugar. Overconsumption of this amount of sugar can lead to obesity, diabetes, and heart disease. And as far as building muscle, there are better hydration alternatives than sports drinks.

Sports drinks have never really done much for me except cause me suffering through intestinal discomfort, bloating, and diarrhea. Since my twenties, I have avoided them. You can see on the ingredient lists of sports drinks that they are packed with items that your body doesn't need, despite the claims of the big-money sponsors of the sports drink campaigns. I found that I am particularly sensitive to food dyes, which have been linked to cancer, ADHD, and allergies. They are synthetic, not natural, and certainly *not* designed for the human body.

You may be tempted by sports drinks (like Red Bull) promoted as *energy drinks*. Be aware that these often contain very high levels of caffeine and other stimulants, as well as huge amounts of sugar. They do not provide the kind of sustained energy you need for athletic competition, and can have exactly the opposite effect by causing poor sleep, crashing when the caffeine wears off, and nutrient-wasting, by stealing your appetite from healthy foods and fluids.

Stimulant use can lead to:

- Dependence
- Nervousness
- Anxiety
- Tremors
- Rapid heartbeat

Stimulants have even been known to lead to death in rare cases. Energy drinks can also cause significant dehydration, as well as raising your blood pressure. You should avoid them at all costs.

Here is the bottom line: There is no big difference between regular soda pop and sports drinks. Don't be a victim of marketing tricks, sponsorships, and advertising slogans that imply sports drinks belong to a different category. You only need to look at the ingredients to see the truth.

So, with all the hype, how do we figure out which choice is the best?

The right answer is — don't drink any of them at all.

If attaining the highest level of performance, wellness, clarity, and vitality are your goals, don't reach for the colorful brands and ingest drinks full of processed sugar and questionable chemicals. Go for basic natural food sources. Water, especially alkalizing water, is our best zero-calorie sports drink. Another healthy alternative would be all-natural coconut water.

The multi-billion dollar business model of using the athlete as a platform for marketing will always be around. However, you don't have to give in to the false programming just because a product uses your sport or because an agent offers you incentives and hooks you up for the almighty dollar.

Make an effort to consider carefully the decisions and choices you make. Like anything else, proper nutrition is all about being smart about your choices. Support pure and natural options that provide your body with the best fuel sources. They are readily available. Take good care of yourself.

Nutrition and Supplementation

Proper nutrition helps the body guard against inflammation and supports recovery. There are specific nutrients that are particularly beneficial. For an athlete, eating well is essential. I also believe supplementation is critical to gaining an edge in athletics. Performance enhancement scandals have given the practice of supplementation a negative connotation. I'm simply talking about supplementation as indulging in items such as fresh squeezed organic juices and homemade smoothies in addition to taking additional vitamins and minerals in the form of a capsule, chewable or powder.

The bioavailability of the nutrients in supplements is 100 percent, compared to food, which is very unpredictable. Overall, you can no longer count on vegetables and fruit to be the packages of concentrated nutrients they once were. At a time when most people aren't coming close to getting five—let alone nine—servings of fruits and vegetables per day, it seems pointless to ask them to eat more to get the same nutrients.

Supplements have proven their worth in scientific studies.

Many diseases can either be prevented by, or ameliorated by, the right nutrients given in supplement form, including:

- Cancer
- Heart disease
- Bone loss
- Stroke
- Macular degeneration

You simply want to increase your vitamins and minerals. Over the long term, the benefits can really add up.

Supplementing your already healthy diet with vitamins and minerals can benefit you through:

- Increased performance
- Increased vitality
- Decreased chances for any diseases down the road
- Increased longevity

Supplements now come in many easy-to-use forms; pills, tabs to dissolve in your water, or ground-up powders.

Maintaining proper nutrition practices to prevent

inflammation will lead to a more pain-free life down the road. Looking back on my own journey, it's the preventative approaches with which I managed my pain and inflammation that led me to having a forty-plus-year-old body that behaves more like a twenty-year-old today.

My top supplement recommendations for vitality, recovery and inflammation are:

- Turmeric (curcumin)
- Green juices and smoothies
- Vitamin D-3
- Resveratrol
- Reishi mushrooms
- Garlic
- Onion
- Cucumber
- Broccoli
- Kale
- Celery
- Lemon and lime
- Spirulina
- Chlorella
- Ginger
- Parsley
- Omega-3 fatty acids

PROPER FOOD AS FUEL

All food is *not* created equal. I have experienced both sides of the spectrum (eating the right foods and the wrong foods).

Now optimum nutrition is my priority:

- To improve physical performance
- To increase mental clarity
- To enhance recovery
- To promote emotional well-being

There is so much information available on diet and nutrition, it is easy to feel overwhelmed, if not confused.

A large part of my effort in advising my athlete clientele is devoted to nutrition education. To begin with, it is important to realize that in order to achieve total wellness and vitality, your awareness needs to be shifted from being a victim to taking full responsibility. The bottom line is this: By and large, the food industry as a whole is *not* interested in your health, but rather, your money.

You have been manipulated, misinformed and led to believe that you are eating real food sources. Let me tell you, a chemically engineered ingredient created in a laboratory is *not* nutrition! Just read *Fast Food Nation* by Eric Schlosser (Houghton Mifflin, 2001) to understand more.

I urge you to take the extra steps in honoring your body as well as the environment. Become a consciously aware consumer. Think carefully about your choices even though it takes a little more time.

Isn't it worth the effort?

It seems like an easy choice, when your performance, health, and well-being are at risk. Look at the bigger picture.

I look at it this way: by supporting a destructive and dishonest system, I am cheating my gifts and my life. A destructive pattern of choices leads to nothing but negative consequences.

It goes without saying that what you put in your body is all about chemistry. You are a living, breathing, biological being. So whatever you put into your body is going to have a profound effect one way or another. Negative or positive, there will be a reaction.

There are good reasons to take the extra steps and buy strictly organic and locally fresh produce. I recommend shopping at your local farmers' market, organic store, or eating at farm-to-table concept restaurants. Always being mindful and prepared is essential when it comes to eating for performance.

Plant-Based Diet

I will never forget that on team road trips during my first year in college, we were given five dollars for lunch and ten dollars for dinner.

Honestly, what did they think we were going to eat?

I ate fast food, of course, which for me was a new experience. I could easily have eaten salad, but the first time I went for the burger, fries, and shake. I remember feeling like I was "stuck in sludge" and having to run to the bathroom at half-time. It was a terrible day. With an excess of fatty meat, processed carbohydrates, and sugars sitting in my stomach, my performance was hindered severely. I had one of the most sluggish games I'd ever had, with nothing in the tank to reach for when I needed it.

It was a harsh lesson on how not eating correctly could affect my performance. I don't think I ate any fast food during any other season. I began to understand that there was a correlation between athletic performance and honoring my body by choosing proper food sources.

Plant-based diets are increasingly promoted in the media and have recently gained popularity among athletes. Over the past ten years, I have cut my meat intake by about 95 percent and now I regularly include raw plants and green juices in my diet.

I can honestly say that my physical condition is better now than it was twenty years ago. Thankfully, there has been a recent expansion of consciousness about diet and nutrition in the sports world; increasing numbers of athletes are changing to plant-based diets. The more you learn about the differences between plants and animals as food, the more sense it will make to you.

Contrary to popular belief, we simply are not designed to eat meat; our bodies have evolved and can no longer process meat efficiently.

If we're not designed to eat meat, why do we?

It is simple; we have been conditioned to eat meat. We are conditioned to believe that animal flesh is good for us and that we were meant to consume it.

I learned a great deal about physiology when I was a pre-med student.

It would probably surprise you to know the following:

- For most of human history mankind has actually lived on a vegetarian diet.

- The human body can absorb plant matter and turn it into top-grade fuel much more quickly than processed foods and meat.

- Saliva in humans is not as acidic as that of flesh-eating or preying animals and this more alkaline saliva does not act as efficiently on meat.

- Our stomach acid isn't strong enough to fully digest meat.

- Meat putrefies within four hours after consumption and, in people, the remnants can cling to the walls of the intestines for months or even years.

- The intestines of carnivores measure about five feet long and are not twisted and turned like the human intestine, which is approximately twenty feet long.

All omnivorous and carnivorous animals eat their meat raw. When a lion kills for food, it tears right into the stomach area to eat the organs that are filled with blood. While eating the internal organs, the lion laps the blood in the process of eating the dead animal's flesh. Even bears that are omnivores eat salmon and other fish raw. If a deer is burned in a forest fire a carnivorous animal will not eat its flesh. Even circus lions have to be feed raw meat or they will not eat.

If humans were truly meant to eat meat then we would eat all of our meat raw and bloody. However, just the thought of eating such meat disgusts us. This is why we must cook it, and then season it with a slew of condiments (ketchup, mayo, mustard, hot sauce, etc.) just to make the taste of the flesh palatable.

Our consumption of meat has created a large industry that includes ranchers, slaughterhouses, and meat-processing plants. Unfortunately, livestock production has a dramatic impact on the environment.

The meat industry is now considered by many to be a leading contributor to global warming. Meat is not economically viable; it takes up to sixteen pounds of grain to produce just one pound of animal flesh. A huge amount of land is required to graze livestock and to grow the grain necessary to feed them. When you consider the collateral damage to the planet (soil erosion, desertification, and threats to indigenous species), it is clear that the land could be put to much better use.

Killing an animal with respect and dignity, as hunters did out of necessity in the past, is quite different from growing animals industrially with no basic rights (fresh air, clean water, space, and so on). Poor living conditions, combined with slaughter methods that are at best cruel, but usually amount to torture, are bound to have negative consequences.

When animals are slaughtered, fear and aggression enzymes are produced and end up in their muscle tissue. Some yoga practitioners abstain from meat because of this. Besides the rotting meat, they simply don't wish to ingest all of the negative emotions from the animal. They feel that these emotions remain in the meat until the consumer ingests the flesh and, in turn, may adopt the same emotions. Fruits and vegetables do not have emotions; therefore, they do not release any emotional chemicals prior to being harvested. The enzymes within fruits and vegetables supply the body with nutrients that will support a healthy state of body and mind.

In recent years, athletes have become more aware of the health benefits of being a vegetarian. If you think that not eating meat is going to make you look scrawny or unhealthy, just consider how densely muscular horses, cows, goats, gorillas, elephants, and rhinoceroses are. They are all herbivores. They also have a longer life span compared to the meat-eating carnivores.

Many meat eaters believe that meat is the only good source of protein. In actuality, the quality of this protein is so poor that little of it can ever be used by humans. This is due to an incomplete combination of amino acids (the building blocks of protein). The excessive amount of protein (the average American eats five times the necessary amount of protein) in a meat-eater's diet is unhealthy for humans.

The large intake of fats from a diet high in meat can result in having a high level of blood cholesterol. Another important health issue related to diet is colon cancer. This form of cancer has become quite common and is triggered by the slow evacuation and putrefaction of meat in the colon. Lifelong vegetarians have a significantly lower risk of such an illness.

What is wellness?

It is often defined backwards; it shouldn't just be about avoiding sickness, it should be about how to feel fantastic.

To digest meat takes a lot of work for little energetic reward. Of course there are many people who eat meat and avoid sickness; there's no disputing that. However, I know from personal experience that it's possible to feel even more incredible when you switch from meat to a vegetarian diet. After eating a vegetarian diet your body will be lighter — possibly in terms of weight, but also think in terms of light energy or photons. Your body actually contains the light energy from the plants you eat.

The reason we eat is to gain energy, which on this planet ultimately comes from the sun. When you eat a plant-based diet, you are getting that sunlight: plants absorb the sun's energy and photosynthesis occurs. When you eat the plant you absorb the energy and feel amazing. When you eat a meat-based diet, you are getting second-hand sunlight.

There are many more benefits associated with becoming a raw vegan or vegetarian than there are for staying a meat eater. I was a Midwestern Ohioan raised on meat and potatoes. I believed I had to eat meat and potatoes to get my bulk of nutrition, particularly protein, as an athlete. Unfortunately, it was not until after my career that I explored the benefits of a raw diet.

At thirty-six years old, on a largely raw vegan diet, I was able to run a sub-four minute mile. Changing your diet to raw and vegan can do wonders for your mind, body and spirit.

Every top achiever I have ever met or read about abstains from a diet of meat. For further insight into this journey follow Rich Roll (blog and podcasts available at richroll.com), and watch the documentaries *Forks Over Knives* (Fulkerson, 2011) and *Food Inc.* (Kenner et al, 2009).

Looking back, as a meat eater my immune system was consistently compromised. I was tired and sluggish, and had constant brain fog, delayed recovery, felt bloated and had countless episodes of an upset gastro-intestinal tract. At the time, I thought everything was normal because it was all I was used to.

In the end, you are robbing yourself of your life potential if you are not prepared to eat correctly and do not provide a proper fuel source for your body. You are doing yourself a great disservice and are actually working against the natural flow of life.

You are what you eat. You've probably heard that before and there is truth in the cliché. However, it doesn't just refer to your physical self. It is deeper; it refers to every aspect of you. What you eat is reflected in your thoughts, your desires, your senses, your emotions, and your deepest self. It is in every aspect of your consciousness. You are, quite literally, what you eat. Don't cheat yourself out of a vibrant, healthy lifespan.

Hydration

Since our bodies are composed of 70 percent water, it goes without saying that hydration is essential. Hydration is one of those things that can easily be ignored, but if you do, the result can be disastrous over time.

Lack of hydration can lead to:

- Muscle cramps
- Decreased muscle performance
- Mental sluggishness

- Injury
- Susceptibility to illness

Something slightly debilitating like a muscle cramp can only lead to greater injuries, which can harm you as an athlete and affect your mobility later in life. Hydration is so easily available; carry a water bottle wherever you go and refill it when it is empty. Consider it a priority.

Things like coffee, soda, energy drinks and alcohol are only going to work against you in achieving your optimal hydration state. They do not provide the kind of sustained energy you need for athletic competition, and can have exactly the opposite effect.

Some of the effects consumption of these drinks can cause are:

- Lack of sleep
- Low energy
- Nutrient-wasting (by stealing your appetite for healthy foods and fluids)

The caffeine in energy drinks, coffee, and soda can also cause:

Significant dehydration

- Increased heart rate
- Increased blood pressure

These are three things you should avoid at all costs on game day and during the season.

Create alkalizing water by adding lemon or lime. It's one of those simple steps that will benefit you in endless ways; research the benefits. It purifies, stimulates, and liquefies bile while inhibiting excess bile flow. It aids digestion; the liver produces more enzymes from lemon and lime water than any other food.

The higher or more alkaline your pH, the more your inner landscape is resistant to minor and major disease. The lemon and lime help bowels eliminate naturally and easily. They are high in potassium, an important mineral that works with sodium for smooth electrical transmission in the brain and nervous system.

Low potassium levels in the blood can lead to problems such as:

- Depression
- Anxiety
- Fogginess
- Forgetfulness

The nervous system needs potassium to assure steady signals to the heart. Calcium and magnesium are also plentiful in a healthy ratio in lemon/lime water. Magnesium is important for heart health and calcium prevents rickets. Even if you drink it before a meal, it will help your body maintain a higher pH than if you didn't drink it at all. Lastly, it reduces phlegm and helps dilute uric acid, which if allowed to accumulate can cause arthritic joint pain.

Sugars

I could write volumes on this topic. Speaking from experience, refined sugars are the ultimate health and performance killers. Anything made from white, refined sugars is going to adversely affect your health, wellness and performance.

There is nothing more disturbing to me than seeing athletes feeding themselves large quantities of sugary treats. Artificial sugar is also unhealthy, but chowing down on too much of the real thing has severe consequences.

Although prime athletes can afford to take in more calories than the average individual, this doesn't mean they can get away with a diet of donuts, candy and ice cream. Not a single athlete gets to the top of their game and stays there by starting his day off with a big bowl of sugary cereal with chocolate and marshmallows.

These refined sugars:

- Overstimulate your pancreas, which is one of the most sensitive organs in your body

- Cause a spike in insulin, priming your body to store more fat

- Cause a spike in blood glucose that will set you up for an energy crash

You know that feeling of having a burst of energy followed quickly by sluggish muscle function and the feeling that you've suddenly hit a wall?

This is the exact scenario that we dread as athletes, and is easy to prevent. In order to do so, we need to learn to reduce refined sugar and maintain a healthy balance of nutrients within our body.

Disease

What do you think of when you hear the word *disease*?

If you take the word apart you can understand its true meaning. If you are in a state of dis-ease, your body, mind and spirit are in a state of **dis** (apart/separate) and **ease** (well-being). Disease is not simply something that suddenly attacks you out of thin air; it is something that develops when your well-being is disrupted over time.

We usually don't identify it until there are medical symptoms, but by that time, the lack of well-being has probably already been around for a while.

Seeing disease from this perspective can help you more effectively address the chronic medical conditions that may affect you:

- Heart disease
- Stroke
- Cancer
- Diabetes
- Arthritis
- Obesity
- Respiratory diseases
- Oral conditions

For the most part, it takes years of practicing unhealthy behaviors to become ill:

- Lack of consistent exercise
- Smoking
- Drinking
- Poor eating choices

This might sound a little cold-hearted. Of course there are exceptions. There are those born with a rare genetic disorder or struck down by a calamity through no fault of their own; I have a truly compassionate heart for those types of circumstances. What I am talking about are the millions of others who court disaster by creating the proper environment for disease to manifest and affect the quality of their lives.

Once disease or injury has set in, there exists an even greater problem: prescription drugs. A multibillion-dollar industry, manufactured prescription drugs are *more* dangerous than illicit drugs. Deaths in the United States via prescription drugs have reached an all-time high. I vehemently oppose these drugs and encourage everyone to do the same.

Even when taken as recommended, prescription and over-the-counter drugs that are meant to treat specific symptoms have side effects that cause more harm than good. We have all been brainwashed and programmed by an industry that has made billions of dollars by fooling us into believing otherwise. Almost 70 percent of Americans take at least one prescription drug, and more than half take two, according to researchers at the Mayo Clinic and Olmsted Medical Center.

What do I know about this problem?

I have experienced the brainwashing firsthand. I have been well acquainted with the medical community since birth, and for much of the first thirty years of my life.

To start with, I was born two months premature and my mother and I had a near death experience. During my childhood I was in and out of doctors' offices all the time. Over the years, doctors wanted to give me more drugs than I can count. Thank God for my parents, who declined over and over when pediatricians wanted to pump my body full of Ritalin and other experimental mind-warping drugs that cause more harm than good.

I have stories that could fill a separate book on this topic but the message I want to give you is: *be skeptical.* Prescription drugs are not the key to wellness. They will not take you where you want to go.

When you are a young athlete, disease might seem like a foreign concept. Overtraining and poor habits will catch up to you eventually; it is important to take care of yourself while you are young. For athletes, the daily grind of training will add up to millions of steps, jumps, or hops. Your body will experience a lot of impact. Orthopedists have never before seen so many joint replacements performed. I believe this has to do with a combination of poor nutritional habits and increased incidence of overtraining beginning at a young age.

"A Porsche doesn't run on fast food" is one of my favorite personal mottos.

Burn it into your mind.

You would never put a poor fuel source into a prime machine, so why dishonor the machine you live in and depend on for your very life?

You can't put garbage and sludge into your body and expect positive results. Eat great and you will feel great.

Your performance, wellness, vitality and longevity are dependent upon your choices.

Do you want to be thin, light, and happy or slow, heavy, inflamed, and moody?

Take the first step and be accountable for yourself. Plan and eat according to exactly how you want to feel and look. It's always your choice.

Remember, disease cannot exist in an alkaline state. If you're suffering from any sort of disease it's because your body is too acidic. You've got to balance your pH. Juicing lemon, lime, or celery is one way of doing it. Plus, they contain anti-cancer compounds so they fight cancer on two fronts. When you are in an alkalized state you don't desire sweets, so this strategy also helps with weight loss.

The chemical compounds in celery, for instance:

- Tell your nervous system to relax
- Lower blood pressure
- Balance your hormones
- Clear up your skin — as crazy as that sounds
- Benefit your kidneys.

PERFORMANCE AND ENERGY

I have never met an athlete who didn't want to have more energy. The more energy you have stored up through your recovery processes, the better performance you are going to have. When it comes down to the key moment in a game, you'll want to find your energy reserves when you reach for them. Energy is something that every athlete tries to maximize. For all of us, no matter what our circumstances, it is the one thing that makes us feel young, vibrant, and alive.

Rest

Rest is the only scientifically proven way that the brain can repair itself. Rest for an athlete should last a minimum of seven hours. Everyone is different; most athletes actually need more than seven hours of sleep to fully recuperate. You need to plan for this. It is so common to encounter athletes who don't ever learn to do this. Invariably, on the nights that they don't rest enough, they won't have the energy, strength, or mental clarity they need the next day to sustain their performance. It is simply because they haven't gotten the proper rest in order to recover from the day before.

The sleep schedule is very important. An athlete might think she can be out until 2:00 a.m. and then expect to get by if she sleeps for close to seven hours. It doesn't work that way. An athlete needs to be in bed no later than eleven o'clock and within three hours postgame. A very strict sleep routine needs to be instilled, especially during the season.

A lack of sleep can alter your vital hormone capabilities, in particular causing a reduction in recovery hormones that aid in muscular growth and repair, such as testosterone and growth hormones. This will lead not only to producing more cortisol, thus an increase in body fat, but will also slow your recovery, and any gains in strength, endurance, or muscular development will be sacrificed.

All in all, sleeping habits and rest can truly make an enormous difference to an athlete.

To improve your sleep, be consistent and follow this routine:

- Go to bed and wake at the same time every day.

- Turn off all electrical devices two hours prior to bed and use natural light in your room.

- Write in your journal; do your daily reflections.

- Draw your curtains at bedtime and keep your bedroom dark.

- Drink a chamomile tea with valerian; these two herbs have been traditionally used for centuries to promote relaxation and sleep. Valerian and chamomile can also help calm occasional anxiety, nervousness, and restlessness. *As with any herbal treatment, consult a certified herbalist to determine the appropriate dosage. Prolonged use of valerian root can cause side effects.*

Start an evening ritual tonight. Getting off your devices might be the most difficult part of this routine, but it is necessary.

Dietary Fats

Does eating fat make you fat?

It sounds logical. For many years diet experts believed that dietary fat caused obesity and so did I. Some experts still believe this despite compelling evidence that eating a fairly high-fat diet is no more likely to cause obesity than eating a high-carbohydrate or high-protein diet. When I was twenty, there was a span of months during which I tried to cut out all fats from my diet and I became very sick as a result. I was lethargic and weak and my immune system became compromised. Fundamentally, I was starving my body. Fat is a necessary component of a healthy diet.

The American Dietetic Association and the American College of Sports Medicine recommend that athletes get 20 to 35 percent of their calories from fat. It is now recognized that many athletes can perform equally well at a varied range of fat intake levels. Some individual athletes may need to experiment before they find their most beneficial range, which may vary during the different stages of training.

Dietary fats have multiple functions in the body in addition to their use as an energy source. Omega-3 fatty acids are especially important for athletes as they help minimize muscular inflammation, thus promoting recovery. Conversely, a diet low in omega-3 fats, even if high in the more common omega-6 fats, can bias your body towards inflammation, impeding exercise recovery.

Integrating fat into your diet does not mean succumbing more often to double bacon cheeseburgers. Omega-6 fats are very common in the modern diet; they can be found in most vegetable and nuts.

Foods rich in omega-3 fats include:

- Walnuts
- Cold-water fish such as salmon
- Flaxseed
- Soybeans
- Soybean oil
- Tofu
- Canola oil

Many experts recommend eating no more than four to five times the amount of omega-6 fats as omega-3 fats.

It's imperative to know the differences in the fats you consume.

Saturated fats are found primarily in animal sources like:

- Meat
- Egg yolks
- Yogurt
- Cheese
- Butter
- Milk

This type of fat is often solid at room temperature. Saturated fat has been linked to health problems such as obesity, high cholesterol, and heart disease. Because of this, saturated fat should be limited to no more than 10 percent of total daily calorie intake. Again, just say *no* to fast food.

The type of fats that should be purposely incorporated into the diet are coconut oil, avocado, nuts, seeds, and olive oil. You can replace dairy with coconut milk or almond milk. Adding these kinds of fats will go a long way in restoring the body, increasing energy sources, and reducing inflammation. When I started incorporating the proper fats into my diet, my performance and health increased exponentially.

Coconut oil has many benefits:

- It has been shown to have anti-inflammatory properties.

- Its lauric acid content promotes a strong immune system, a necessity for any high performing athlete or individual looking to take the next step in wellness and vitality.

- Due to its lack of processing, virgin coconut oil contains a high concentration of a form of saturated fat (medium-chain fatty acids), which is absorbed much faster than long-chain fatty acids. These fatty acids are sent straight into circulation—more like a carbohydrate than a fat—and then to the liver to be quickly oxidized. This process makes coconut oil an extremely efficient source of fuel.

Quieting the Nervous System

Whether you are an athlete or a non-athlete, learning to quiet your nervous system can be a valuable skill. It has many beneficial results.

Quieting your nervous system can help to:

- Reduce anxiety
- Increase clarity in the mind
- Reduce stress

All of these changes can lead to increased mental and physical performance.

Understanding the nervous system may seem overwhelming and daunting, I know. But let's put this in more simplistic terms. Think of your autonomic nervous system as being split between training (switch on) and rest/recovery (switch off).

Switch on: It is the sympathetic division of the nervous system that excites. It's known for preparing you for fight or flight.

Switch off: The parasympathetic division, by contrast, inhibits. It's known for allowing you to rest and recover.

Have you heard stories of people lifting cars or achieving superhuman levels of strength during a survival situation?

This is an example of a fight-or-flight response. Knowing when to excite and when to inhibit is crucial to performance. Unfortunately, just knowing this is not enough, because the autonomic nervous system regulates itself unconsciously. It is responsible for regulating automatic activities in your body, like breathing and heartrate.

Most people teeter-totter between sympathetic and parasympathetic control, which is like idling a car. Sure, you're prepared for action, but you're not going anywhere. Even though you may not be moving, the engine is still *on* and eventually you will run out of gas. You will pay a price because you won't get anything accomplished on empty.

Although this directly relates to training, I'm talking about your life environment as well. It's easy to keep your nervous system hyped up with nonstop technology, music, parties, and other overstimulating diversions.

I was one of those who thought being fired up before a game was a good thing, but you actually want to be as calm as possible before a game. This takes a lot of training as our species has been wired for war by many thousands of years of survival under duress.

I have found that, because of the constant overstimulation of the modern lifestyle, athletes aren't even aware when they reach a fight-or-flight state. That is hyperactivity of the nervous system. The intensity of a training regimen causes athletes to be in a constant state of increased hormones and feel-good chemicals. It is easy to become accustomed to that state because it feels good, but many athletes don't know how to manage the intensity, and over the long term it can lead to addiction or depression.

Many of the top, world-class athletes and top tier collegiate athletes have prevailing parasympathetic nervous systems, which gets them into trouble because, to a coach, it appears as they are slacking off during practice. But if they're good enough to compete with the rest of the team while only playing at 80 percent of their capabilities, they might not engage the fight-or-flight system to gain the extra 20 percent.

These athletes are the exception, however. It is much more common for athletes to have a problem with overstimulation; they spend too little time in rest and recovery and exist in a constant state of over-arousal and overtraining.

High intensity training has a big impact on the central nervous system and can take weeks, if not months, to recover from. This is why athletes who must peak annually will struggle to reproduce personal best performances for any extended period of time.

Here are some symptoms of overtraining:

- You train harder but your output decreases.
- You lose motivation.
- You are sick more often.
- Your heart rate goes up.
- You experience chronic soreness.
- You have pain in joints, bones, and limbs.
- You feel sluggish all day.
- You lose focus and become restless.

Do any of these sound familiar?

If so, it is important to address the issues before it brings you into a downward spiral of performance and health.

Turning yourself off is just as important as turning yourself on. Do things that disengage you from reality, allowing your parasympathetic nervous system to kick in more easily.

Some athletes play video games. After practice, they go home, rest, and play the games to escape from it all. It might seem like this is a restful practice, but it is an illusion, especially if you are huddled around in a group shouting and competing. I recommend choosing a less stimulating escape, like reading a book or writing in a journal.

Personally, I have found that the best way to quiet the nervous system is to get physically away from the training environment.

Here are some guidelines and ideas:

- Purposely set aside time for yourself to be quiet.

- Each quiet period should be at least a half-hour in duration.

- Get away from distractions.

- Go for a walk in nature or just sit outside and get some fresh air.

- Go for a swim.

- Leave your cell phone behind and do not listen to music.

- If you are indoors, turn off all electronics: phone, television, music, computer.

I can't stress enough how important these quiet periods are.

There are additional strategies and therapies that may help regenerate the nervous system. Choose what works for you.

Some of them are listed below:

- Massage
- Breath work
- Trigger point therapy
- Rolfing
- Reiki
- Energy therapy
- Water therapies
- Ice baths
- Whirlpools
- Saunas and steam rooms
- Power naps

- Limiting or completely removing caffeine and other stimulants from your diet

CHAPTER THREE

Body

FLEXIBILITY

Working on flexibility is just as important as any other type of training because it helps us gain better range of motion throughout the body. This is only going to complement your performance, prevent injury, and enhance recovery rate for muscles and joints. Furthermore, the more flexibility we can gain at a younger age, the better off we will be in our later years.

While most athletes will say they understand how important flexibility is, they often won't set aside time to do the exercises. In a busy life, when it is hard to fit everything in, flexibility training is one of the most commonly neglected tasks. It should be one of the most stressed components of an athlete's regimen.

To enhance flexibility, include dynamic stretching in your warm-ups and save static stretching exercise for post workout. Focus on the shoulder joint, the hip, your squatting form, and your ankle movement.

I highly recommend finding someone that can help you identify your tightest areas through a screening process so you can focus your work on them. It is important to vary your stretching routines—it helps to reduce boredom and also makes your exercises more effective over the long-term. Practicing yoga will enhance all areas of flexibility.

Yoga

I wish I had discovered yoga at a younger age than I actually did. It helped to heal my very broken-down, inflamed, injured, chronically sore, and painful body and it revitalized me, body and mind. Afterwards, doctors considered me twenty-five to thirty years younger. I am living proof of the wondrous healing and balancing power of yoga.

Yoga is a simple, but powerful, practice of connecting the mind to the body through breath and movement. I believe that every athlete should incorporate yoga into their daily routine.

Yoga practice offers may benefits:

- Yoga poses will help to improve balance.
- Yoga stretches will increase flexibility.
- Yoga helps repair and recover of body damage.
- Yoga is meditative and helps to decrease the distracting chatter in an athlete's mind.

All of these factors will result in an improvement of athletic performance.

I first heard of yoga in my youth from the legend, Kareem Abdul Jabbar, arguably one of the greatest to ever play the game of basketball.

Kareem said, "Basketball is a sport of endurance and you have to know how to control your breath, the very essence of yoga, too. Therefore, I intentionally started using yoga techniques in my play. Once I began to practice it, I did not suffer from any muscle injuries in the rest of my career. Yoga has aided me to alleviate the number as well as severity of injuries. As a preventative medicine, it's matchless."

His successful basketball career spanned twenty years — one of the longest careers in professional sports.

As Kareem famously said, "I can do more than stuff a ball through a hoop. My biggest asset is my mind."

In yoga practice, it is said that all obstacles are in the mind. The work you do on yourself to find peace does not involve changing your circumstances. It starts with accepting your circumstances, and accepting who and where you are.

The integration of mind and body are intricately linked, each influencing the other down to behavior on a cellular level. Emotions trigger the release of special compounds known as peptides, which are stored by the body, in a tissue, organ or muscle. So, unexpressed emotions are literally lodged in the body, waiting to be brought to consciousness and worked on. These emotions need to be expressed and integrated into the whole person; this is part of the process of healing. A yoga practice can open the door for you to stop clinging to old thought patterns and beliefs, and release emotions that are stored in the body. Then you can become truly free.

Recovery

Recovery has to be one of the most misunderstood processes of the entire athletic scheme. The amount of information and misinformation available to athletes can be overwhelming. It is actually very simple.

Without the proper fuel sources, exercise-induced damage to your muscles inhibits strength and endurance. The microscopic damage from training causes inflammation. Simply put, inflammation is an immune system response to tissue damage. It functions to remove cellular debris from the site of damage and initiate repair. When muscles are inflamed, they are typically sore and also lose strength and range of motion. *Recovery* is the term that describes the recuperation of muscles following this kind of damage. It is an ongoing process for an athlete.

How do you promote recovery?

- Sleep promotes recovery.

- Rest promotes recovery (and by rest, I mean *real* downtime to relax and repair the nervous system).

- Hydration and proper nutrition are vital for recovery.

- Omega-3 fatty acids especially assist by reducing inflammation.

- I have also found that taking time for reflection and quietude and solitude positively impacts many aspects of training, including recovery.

Don't sacrifice everything for the sake of performance. Let me make this clear: the goal should be to prioritize life and maximize performance without personal sacrifice. We are human, it is psychologically healthy to sometimes kick back, relax, and enjoy an evening out with friends. I'm not suggesting you must live a militant life to achieve amazing results.

Sometimes, and you will recognize when it is needed, just allow yourself to unwind, and celebrate your meat or fish and have a glass of whatever you rarely have to drink. Life for an athlete who sacrifices everything for the sake of performance can very lonely and tiresome. Seek balance instead.

Focusing a little more on rest and recovery can pay exponential dividends beyond additional training time. Risk of injury will decrease and it is likely that your sleep, as well as your general sense of well-being, will improve. If you ignore your body's recovery needs, the opposite will be true. There is nothing worse to an athlete than having to take unnecessary time off due to an injury, burnout, or something debilitating that could have been prevented.

The more you support your body during recovery, the longer a career you will be able to have and the longer a lifespan you may have as well. A balanced combination of rest and recovery along with proper diet and exercise should be a part of any fitness regimen.

Joint Care

For an athlete, joints should be treated like objects of great value, like the house, car, or yacht of your dreams. They are priceless and require great care and attention.

You can take several steps to protect and support your joints:

- Don't train on concrete or asphalt surfaces.
- Take care not to overtrain.
- Be sure to get proper nutrition.
- Maintain good hydration.
- Use ice after training when necessary.

- Support joint recovery after training.
- Do regular stretching and flexibility exercises.
- Begin a yoga practice.

A proper joint flexibility program should be incorporated on a daily basis.

I have found this process to be the best way to do this:

1. Warm up your body first for fifteen minutes.
2. Do flexibility exercises.
3. Afterwards, continue with the rest of your training regimen.

Stretch after each training session, and then stretch again lightly at the end of the night. Don't neglect your joints; taking care of them can make a huge difference. Your body will always be limber and injuries will be reduced. Your athletic performance will only improve.

SPORT-SPECIFIC TRAINING

World-class athletes like Olympians have very specific training regimens, designed for the particular movements required by their sport. You can't expect to become a world-class sprinter if you're lifting like a body builder and running like a long-distance runner.

As you rise through different levels of performance you will have to create more specific training plans in order to advance in your sport. Without a well-thought out plan, you will not achieve your goals.

Athleticism

Athleticism is a term used to describe an athlete who can move with grace and efficiency in ways that most people can't. For example, the athleticism of Michael Jordan was remarkable because of the things he could do with his body that had never been seen before. His execution of athletic movements at optimum speed with precision, style, and grace in the realm of basketball was like that of a dancer.

There are natural athletes, but it is possible to increase your athleticism by design. It's all about choosing appropriate training. Here are some ideas:

- Chose activities that work on particular components of movements that you want to improve. For example, working on balance alone will increase athleticism.

- Yoga improves flexibility, muscle control, grace, balance and breathing.

- Practice active art forms like dancing.

- Play another sport for fun, choosing one that will incorporate different movement patterns to complement the movements of your sport. Some of the greatest athletes are dual-sport athletes.

- Add an activity that improves hand-eye coordination.

- Add a variety of movements to your training; jumping, dragging something, agility ladders, wind sprints, shuffling, lateral movement, changing directions, reaching, or pulling.

How many movements does your current training regimen incorporate?

Add some more to enhance your training.

Variation

Variation refers to changes in program and training over specific time periods. It is also referred to as *periodization*. Most comparative studies I researched for my master's thesis have demonstrated the superiority of periodized over non-periodized programs in terms of greater enhancement of strength, body composition, and motor performance.

When variety is not incorporated into training, consequences like overtraining and adrenal fatigue can result. This is why world-class athletes and colleges often use periodized training. The goal of this variation is to maximize your gains while also reducing your risk of injury, burnout, overtraining or illness over the period of a year.

This system of training is typically divided up into three or four types of cycles.

Trainers or athletes may break the year into quarters:

- Pre-season
- In-season
- Post-season
- Recovery-season

A pre- or post-season cycle may be anywhere from two weeks to a few months and can further be classified into different phases:

- Preparation phase
- Competition phase
- Peaking phase
- Transition phase

The variation in training gives the nervous system time to adapt or rest, allows the stimulation of various muscles through different exercises, and it may also give the body certain amounts of rest that it needs.

A good variation program will be well planned to address your specific training needs while maintaining the skills that you have worked so hard to build.

Weak Points

The saying, "You're only as strong as your weakest link" is absolutely true.

Every athlete that I have ever trained or known is definitely aware of their weak point; however, many athletes I've trained have had difficulty working on them effectively.

Weakness is nothing to be embarrassed about; there is no perfect athlete. Learning to work on your weaknesses will make you a better athlete. In addition, learning to accept and work on our weak points is going to benefit us in other areas of life as well. It is a life skill that will make us able to face any obstacle and improve ourselves, which is the key to evolving in life.

My favorite author, Ernest Hemingway, said, "If you want to be a writer, then go home and start writing."

That is almost the same analogy for if you want to be a great basketball player: Go home and work specifically on basketball. Whatever sport you want to be great at, don't talk about it, *do* it.

Sport-specific training is exactly that. It takes many concentrated hours to become great at anything. A beginner must put in a huge amount of effort to before they can hope to reach a level of excellence. At some point, however, you reach a certain skill level and simply repeating the same pattern again and again doesn't foster much additional growth.

Anders Ericsson, the psychologist behind the 10,000-Hour Rule, explained this important caveat by saying, "You don't get benefits from mechanical repetition, but by adjusting your execution over and over to get closer to your goal. You have to tweak the system by pushing, allowing for more errors at first as you increase your limits."

The same thing applies to life. You can't expect to have exponentially profound results if you're not willing to be specific about what it is your goals are. You have to know what you want and then take specific actions to achieve it.

LONGEVITY

No matter what level they areat, every athlete wants to avoid injury, illness, pain, and any debilitating disease. Longevity is something that needs to be considered during a career. Think about the athlete's body; our joints and organs are being more or less abused during the entire process of a career. You should start thinking about long-term goals now.

Legacy

I am thinking of impact as a mindset and not the physical jarring of the body. In my athletic career I had some really hard lessons, and I've come to understand that less is more. The more we can lessen impact, the better off we are going to be. Less is more. Always feel like you have a little more in the gas tank and just walk away. This is critical and crucial to understand in order to increase and maintain peak performance.

When I think of true impact I think of legacy. If you are making a meaningful, lasting and energizing contribution to humanity by serving a cause greater than your own, then you are leaving a legacy.

The requirements of a legacy are that you embrace your uniqueness, passionately immersing your whole self into life so that your gift will be to all. In leaving a legacy, you take the responsibility to ensure that it will have a life beyond that of you, its creator, outliving and outlasting your time on Earth.

The lens of legacy gives you a view of your life from a generational perspective, where you become aware of the desire to live beyond yourself, focused on making a difference in the lives of others. It is giving back.

Creating your legacy is a pathway resulting in a deep sense of significance, where true meaning is found somewhere beyond the pursuit of success. It results in a ripple effect that positively impacts society. Inherently, when you shift to living your legacy, your influence comes from who you are at the core.

Mindful Breathing

The first process that I work on with any client is gaining control over the breath.

Why is the breath so important?

It is the single most human action or element that consistently represents life. Breath is life. When you focus on the breath, your shift in awareness causes the control of the breath to shift from the brain stem to the cerebral cortex. It is a shift from the subconscious to the conscious. It's in that moment, through intimate awareness, that the magic happens. You will notice your mind slow down (this feels awesome) and you will become calm and quiet as a peaceful consciousness develops.

Many people need to learn to breathe in a healthy way. The better we can learn to maintain our breath, especially under stress, in which we tend to hold our breath, the more we can relax. Taking fuller and deeper breaths in the proper manner will reduce stress and increase quality of life, as well as longevity.

I have found that breath has an intimate relationship to life energy throughout the entire body. Breath has everything to do with our structural alignment and the physical muscular patterns of our bodies, at rest and in motion.

There are many benefits to the importance of breath awareness:

- It can eliminate joint compression.

- It can reduce imbalances caused by one's postures and attitudes.

- Awareness of breath is the foundation for flowing seamlessly in movement.

- In this state, emotional stress and random thoughts are less likely to occur.

- The deeper your awareness of your breath is, the better your energy in your body will flow, pushing through any emotional and physical blockages.

- Awareness of breath is freeing to the body and mind.

When the breath moves, the mind follows; the breath gives us a tool with which we can explore the subtler structures of our mental and emotional worlds. When your breath changes, that tells you that something is happening in your mind.

When something happens in your mind, like a disturbing thought, for example, your breath will reflect that back to you. Now you may understand that because the breath and mind are so connected, awareness and mindfulness of breathing can lead to insight into the nature of mind. Insight into the nature of the mind leads eventually to freedom; releasing the past, recovering from emotional trauma, overcoming resentment, discouragement, addiction, or depression.

Over the past five years, as I practiced breath awareness to help in my recovery from PTSD, I have seen the following improvements:

- My emotional health has improved dramatically.
- My relationships have improved.
- My thinking has become clearer than ever.
- My flexibility has increased.
- I am more efficient, so my productivity is greater.
- Under stressful situations I have become less reactive.

The benefits have been truly profound.

Brain Health

With more and more cases of concussion, dementia, and Alzheimer's, awareness of brain health issues has increased in recent decades. We have the power to increase our brain health by making smart lifestyle choices, like good nutrition and regular exercise of body and mind. Leading research has proven that the earlier we start addressing brain health, the less likely we will have debilitating diseases hampering us later in life.

Concussions are a topic of grave concern. Consider an athlete that spends thousands of hours on a stellar career and is unable to even remember it later in life. It is a tragedy and is preventable.

I think high school football players are at particular risk. Today, teen athletes in high schools are the size, strength and ability of those in college forty years ago. Their young developing brains experience repeated high impact collisions that can lead to permanent injury. Impact brain injuries may not show symptoms for many years.

Chronic traumatic encephalopathy, or CTE, was spotted by Dr. Bennet Omalu in an autopsy of NFL Hall of Famer and Steeler center Mike Webster.

Those with CTE have symptoms that include:

- Memory loss
- Confusion
- Disorientation
- Depression
- Negative changes in behavior and decision-making

Incidence rates remain unclear for the progressive disease and symptoms may turn up years after repeated concussions or other head trauma.

Concussion rates among female athletes are highest in soccer players.

A soccer ball doesn't seem dangerous, right?

But if you head away thunderbolt shots or goalkeeper's clearances regularly there is a risk that the brain can suffer repetitive sub-concussive injuries that may have a cumulative effect.

Sub-concussive impacts cause no readily observable symptoms that would indicate injury to the brain; however, in a study at the Human Injury Research and Regenerative Technologies Laboratory at Purdue University it was found that some of these college soccer players had brain injuries as severe as American football players. That should be a wake-up call to skeptics who can't imagine that even a lightweight football can cause significant damage.

My goal and passion as a professional mentor, coach, and trainer is to simply increase awareness of how your decisions will ultimately impact your career and life. I am certainly guilty of not considering longevity or vitality when I was eighteen or twenty. I naturally just wanted to train harder and more intensely. However, the unfortunate reality is our body breaks down over time.

Longevity is not only something that we should consider with respect to our careers but also with respect to the rest of our lives.

What kind of quality of life do you want to have in your later years?

How do you want to feel?

How do you want to look?

Do you want to be able to play with your kids and grandkids, or do you want to be hampered by brain deficits or debilitating joint problems?

Longevity is a serious topic to consider; by practicing preventative approaches and increasing awareness, you will be able to have a healthy, happy career and a longer, more vital life.

CHAPTER FOUR

Surroundings

POSITIVITY

Without positivity, there can be no joy. Positive and negative thinking have a major impact on a person, as well as on the surrounding environment.

During the 1990s, Dr. Masaru Emoto performed a series of experiments observing the physical effect of words, prayers, music, and environment on the crystalline structure of water. Emoto hired photographers to take pictures of water that had been exposed to different variables and was subsequently frozen so that it would form crystalline structures.

The results were nothing short of remarkable. In the photos, the water stamped with positive words is far more symmetrical and organized than that stamped with dark, negative phrases. That concept is relatively easy to grasp, but this extremely tangible evidence of it is astounding. If the words and thoughts that come out of us have this effect on water crystals, it's amazing to think of what kind of effect they have on the people and events that come into our lives.

My favorite example of the power of positivity and the energy associated with it is an experiment with water and rice grains. Both were exposed to negativity, a harsh, lower tone. The water crystals turned dark and irregular, and therefore the rice turned dark; it almost seemed to wither up and crumble.

There has been plenty of evidence that the same could happen on a person's cellular level, causing damage that could lead to debilitating outcomes like depression, addiction, helplessness and suicide. Negativity only leads to suffering.

The need for a new focus on positivity is great in the sports world. Constantly focusing on cutthroat competitiveness, we've lost the ability to enjoy our lives and to tap into internal resources. There should be a return to sportsmanship and enjoyment. Coaches need to be held more accountable for their words. Athletes, too, need to recognize the power in positivity — it can only lead to better performances, balanced bodies, healthier competitions, and an improved quality of life.

Wellness

Wellness is a simple concept. At any given point in life, you are either well or unwell. Think of it as a holistic term; it is a whole-life concept. Too many define wellness as the opposite of being sick, and rely on prescription drugs to return one to wellness (when these drugs are actually one of the leading killers in the United States).

Wellness is a collaborative lifestyle; it's a mindset. It requires constant education and preventative health practice as well as the nurturing of respect and self-love.

Love

The most powerful force in a living, breathing human being is love. It is a natural state but is sometimes difficult to tap into because we have mistaken beliefs, distractions and expectations. It is something you can learn to find.

The Beatles got it right when it comes to love; that *is* what humanity is all about. It is treating our neighbor with compassion, and judging each other kindly. The more we can practice love with each other, the more we offer our souls a higher level of consciousness.

I see love not as a feeling, but as a human amalgamation of intellectual ability, skill, consciousness, and awareness. It is the ability to respond to people, and all of life, with kindness, compassion, and equanimity.

Kindness is the ability and effort to respond to someone in a way that makes them happy. Compassion is the aspiration to understand and help relieve someone of the suffering they experience. Equanimity is the ability to be kind and compassionate to all beings, without bias, whether we like them or not.

In addition to improving our own life, I've realized that if I can uproot selfishness in me, I free myself from suffering. I can also help others to uproot selfishness, be free of suffering and realize true love. If they can do it, they can help others.

Imagine what the world would be like if everyone was free from selfishness and suffering and capable of true love in each moment. There would be no wars, no one would go without food and shelter, and no one would be lonely in moments of pain. Being aware of the fact that each moment I practice mindfulness is taking us one step closer to a world free of suffering makes each moment of my life incredibly meaningful.

Let's also dispel some myths about what it means to love yourself. Self-love is not about being arrogant or egotistical. It is not about comparing yourself to others to determine if you are good enough. It is not about always putting yourself first at the expense of others. It is not about always getting your way. It is not about winning.

To love yourself is to be in awe of the miracle of your existence.

To love yourself means:

- Accepting yourself as you are — the light parts and the dark, the good and the bad — while knowing that the real you is above the perceived dualities of the physical realm

- Being willing to receive as much as you are willing to give

- Knowing your values and your boundaries and honoring them

- Teaching others how to treat you by showing them how you treat yourself

- Being kind to yourself

- Looking after your mind, your body, and your spirit

- Knowing you are worth it, not because of what you have achieved or what you look like or what others think of you, but because *love is your birthright,* no matter what

A simple practice can help you to cultivate self-love:

1. Take a moment to think of those things you

most need to hear from others. It may be that you need to hear that you are loved or admired, or accepted just as you are. You might want to hear that you are appreciated or forgiven.

2. Write them down on a piece of paper. Make sure to exhaust your list. You will find that what you most want to hear from others is what you most need to tell yourself. You should now have a list of positive affirmations tailor-made for you.

3. Repeat these affirmations every day, morning and night, and include them in visualization sessions.

You will soon enjoy a sense of self-love and inner peace that you never had before.

Wealth

Wealth seems to be one of those distorted concepts, which, again, we as a society have been programmed to think about in the wrong way. Much of our perception comes from our family lineage. The Great Depression affected many families and their belief systems, including my own. I inherited a false belief system associated with wealth that I have worked extremely hard to revise.

Wealth is not a monetary issue; it is beyond money. We

are the wealthiest nation in the entire world. We take so much for granted.

Wealth should be about quality, not quantity. Wealth is abundance. Just take a walk outside and look at the trees, look at your surroundings. There is so much we take for granted, so much we don't recognize because we have been accustomed to having so much.

We have become desensitized to our own wealth; we can't see it even though it is all around us. If we can view wealth as more than having things, the level of joy in your immediate environment will automatically be raised multiple levels.

Positivity is strongly related to the concept of wealth. Interestingly, being an elite athlete has made it so I have had to re-train myself to be positive, to feel the wealth around me.

Negative associations become rooted into your neurological system and lead to debilitating things such as destructive behavior, depression, judgment, harshness, and anger. Emotions and behaviors that come out of negativity cause outcomes that will not take us to the higher realm we are seeking.

Positivity takes practice. It takes a lot of compassion and letting go. If it isn't now in your grasp, it should be scheduled into a routine until it is a rediscovered.

Remember, you can never take material possessions with you once your physical life expires, so focus on a different definition of wealth. I promise it will bring you more joy to practice positivity than anything else. Lead with your heart and share the wealth.

LEADERSHIP

Effective leaders are hard to find these days.

What are the qualities of a good leader?

If we just take a look back at leaders who have impacted the world in positive ways, we'll find they have similar qualities. They have compassion, honesty and brevity, and they are unfailingly positive.

I'm talking about people like:

- Gandhi
- Churchill
- Mandela
- Peter the Great
- Martin Luther King, Jr.
- Thomas Jefferson

You can probably think of others.

Are there other qualities you can think of that effective leaders possess?

Which of these leadership qualities do you have?

List the qualities you honor and consider how you can incorporate these into your training rituals.

Like Gandhi said, "Be the change you wish to see in the world."

Good leaders are both compassionate and bold. One of my all-time favorite leaders is someone who is known for never cursing because he claimed that those kinds of words incite a negative vibration and a debilitating environment. The leader I am talking about is John Wooden. The sports world has rarely seen a coach that has encompassed such authentic leadership skills as Coach Wooden. Seriously, if you want to learn about leadership, research and study John Wooden's methodologies. He was truly a world-class leader.

True leaders:

- Know how to get results
- Know how to move people
- Understand the importance of positivity
- Are compassionate and respectful
- Inspire
- Naturally raise their teammates or co-workers to a higher state

A good leader's spirit is contagious and people are naturally drawn closer to them. If you are an athlete who wants to be a champion, and perhaps a good leader as well, think carefully about whom you choose to have around you.

Are you choosing authentic leaders and mentors who will raise you up and make you a better person, as well as a better athlete?

Confrontation

Confrontation is simply the result of two negative forces or beliefs coming together. It's like magnets. When you send out strong negativity, you will inevitably be faced with confrontation on a really negative level.

I have experienced some great lessons about confrontation in my life. I can tell you from personal experience that like attracts like. There is energy associated with positivity, and there is energy associated with negativity. If you can, imagine a radio dial, with different emotions dialed in to different signals. The signal that you send out is what you are going to attract.

Is your signal positive or negative?

It is your choice to make.

The signal you send out is determined by the way you think inside. Think positively and you will radiate positively. Once you figure out how to maintain a more positive signal more positive outcomes are going to come to you.

When a person is negatively tuned and gets involved in a conflict, it invariably results in a confrontation. Sometimes the person is only trying to stand his ground, but they do it in such a negative way that it results in an angry explosion.

I cringe when I hear of athletes that constantly are in the news for making bad decisions and putting themselves into negative situations. The rippling effects on their lives, as well on as their teammate's lives, are significant.

There are strategies to avoid confrontation and to help others to do so as well:

- Stay positive as much as possible; lead by example.

- Stress the importance of remembering that there is always a bigger picture than your own personal perspective.

- Always try to keep your communication with other people positive.

- Make calm word choices and resist negative actions.

Of course, violence in any form — in words or punches or bullets — represents a complete loss of personal control. Nothing positive has ever come from throwing a punch. It never has and never will.

Values

Values define you in many ways:

- They will dictate how you make decisions and how you manage your life.

- They tell the world about your priorities.

- Values define your purpose in the past, present and future.

What do you really stand for at the center of your heart and your soul?

Only you know the answer.

What is most important to you?

Identify and reflect on your values not only on a daily basis, but also on a weekly, monthly, quarterly, and annual basis.

I keep my top five values — what I stand for and what I hold dear to my heart — on a piece of paper and go over them morning and night as part of my rituals. I recommend doing this to stay grounded, to be yourself, and to always know who you are.

Effectiveness: Less is More

Are you an effective athlete?

What does that mean?

Let's look at effectiveness as efficiency. An efficient athlete is one who can perform a maneuver while expending as little energy as possible. It seems like a purely physical concept, but it is a combination of many factors, including focus and awareness. Training for efficiency involves targeting specific goals.

Visualize two light bulbs burning. One of them is an old-fashioned high-wattage bulb and the other is one of those new, ultra-energy-efficient bulbs that uses about a tenth of the energy. You want to be an efficient athlete; you want to be able to shine bright but waste little energy.

Less *is* more; I learned this the hard way. I overtrained for many years, never getting the results that I knew were in me. I didn't understand how to focus on being effective; I only kept training harder. It took a long time to learn how to train without overtraining. Now I know that if you are working effectively, it should always feel as if you have more left in the gas tank at the end of the day.

When you are more efficient:

- You will be more focused.
- You can be more effective as an athlete.
- You will waste less time and energy.
- Your body will be spared unnecessary strain.
- You will increase longevity for our careers and our lives.

Remember, less *is* more.

VIBRATIONS

> *Everything is energy and that's all there is to it. Match the frequency of the reality you want and you cannot help but get that reality. It can be no other way. This is not philosophy. This is physics.*
> ~ attributed to Albert Einstein

There is a realm of study called metaphysics that is finally gaining credibility. Metaphysics explores the vibrational energies of our universe and their effect on humanity. Scientists have proven that a single thought can impact our immediate environment because all life forms, including humans, are energetic beings.

With this in mind, we need to be very aware of our thoughts and their potential impact. I feel a need to stay mindful of the kind of energy I am sending out to the world. It not only impacts my health and my work but it also could disturb the animal world many miles away.

It makes you wonder, doesn't it?

What impact are you making on the world with your thoughts?

Are you sending out positive energy?

Is it having an effect on you and others near you?

Your vibrations may be impacting the world, far and near. Be careful with your thoughts.

Vibration is a tone, a feeling, a mindset. When we find ourselves in a state of doom and gloom, when we are constantly complaining, commiserating, comparing, or cursing, we are practicing a negative vibration. To reach a positive vibration state, we need to lead by practicing positive thoughts, words and actions. Like attracts like, and at the end of the day, if you are in a positive, higher-resonating vibration, I promise you will reach the goals you seek in sports, in relationships, and in life.

Intuition

Intuition is a skill, a primordial awareness. Think of it as your internal global positioning system. When we listen to this internal voice we may be guided to the solutions to life's problems. Our intuition is the human technology with which we receive guidance from an intelligent universe. We all have the ability to access it in varying degrees.

Have you ever heard someone say "...it raised a red flag"?

This is an example of an intuitive experience. It comes without coherent thought, but is a powerful message. It is an inner guide, a higher realm of knowing.

As athletes, it is important to listen to these messages. The more you can tap into your intuition, the better your performance will be as an athlete and the better your outcomes in life will be.

If you want to build your intuition, practicing meditation is key. I can't stress that enough. Developing a practice of mindfulness allows your intuition to blossom simply because it removes all the clutter from your mind that distracts you from hearing your inner voice. Clarity is power — go inward to find it.

Heart Intelligence

We all know what IQ or Intelligence Quotient is.

Have you ever heard of EQ, or Emotional Quotient?

EQ is the intelligence of the heart and I truly believe it is much more powerful than IQ.

Many times I have heard athletes honored by saying, "He has a huge heart," or "He led with his heart."

These are some of the highest compliments you can pay an athlete. Words like these are said about the most admired people in any field.

New research explores the intricacies of heart-brain messaging, how emotions affect human biology and the influences of geomagnetic fields and solar activity on our bodies, including our hearts.

What does all that mean?

If you think about it, the heart is wired with its own system; it is beating to its own electrical rhythm or current. The fact that the heart generates the strongest electromagnetic field produced by the body, coupled with the recent discovery that this field becomes more coherent as the individual shifts to a sincerely loving or caring state, is proof that the field generated by the heart may significantly contribute to much more energy exchange than western medicine has ever credited. It means that the heart has its own intelligence.

We often make the mistake of leading with our ego mind, which leads to undesirable outcomes. Lead from the heart instead.

I still believe that leading with my heart was my strongest asset as an elite athlete, and I urge other athletes to do the same.

Why?

Because you will lead a life of passion. Yes, it takes determination, hard work, sacrifice and faith, but I can tell you that passion equals fulfillment.

Don't make the mistake of thinking that fulfillment is fame or money. I have witnessed athletes who, starting off, tapped into their heart intelligence and made it straight to the top. In response to the fame and money, they changed and started to lead from their ego instead and it all fell apart.

The ego mind likes to control and deceive and make us think that the new sports car, the biggest mansion, and the ego-driven things in life are what we want. They are what big business has engineered us into believing is success. Unfortunately, these things don't bring fulfillment because you only want more.

Practice heart-centered intelligence instead. You have the ultimate power to decide when to start living your life. Your boss, parents, partner or friends can't decide that for you. Only you can. Be brave. Be courageous. Be passionate. Lead from the heart.

The Flow State

Any athlete that has been in the flow state has experienced timelessness. It's almost like everything is put on pause, everything suddenly seems seamless and you can understand and see the whole system laid out clearly. Suddenly things happen with no resistance. This is the flow state.

The flow state results in optimal performance. Athletes like Joe Montana, Michael Jordan, Larry Bird, Magic Johnson, and Andre Agassi — the all-time greats — know how to achieve and practice the flow state. There is a lot of research on flow; I recommend reading as much as you can to practice how to achieve it and how to keep yourself as long as possible in the flow state. Things that will help are breath control and meditation.

Ultra-successful achievers such as Kobe Bryant, Steve Jobs, Madonna, Lebron James, Ray Dalio, Oprah Winfrey, George Lucas, and The Beatles all had personal breakthroughs through meditation; they are known for saying that meditation helped them slow down, relax and reach the flow. Once they were in the flow state, great ideas emerged and personal breakthroughs happened.

It is important to keep in mind that the meditative state cannot be forced. Remember to slow down, relax, and breathe.

CHAPTER FIVE

Relationships

Relationships are vital to our lives as human beings and should be a source of fulfillment and joy. Unless you live in a cave with no access to the outside world, you must learn to manage relationships and it isn't always easy.

Why are we always facing so many relationship crises?

In a modern world, which is so fast-paced, we tend to be locked into our technology and it seems that, perhaps, the art of relating to one another is slowly dwindling away.

I once read an article in which elders in their nineties were asked what they considered the most important aspect of life.

Do you know what they all said?

They all wished they had fostered their relationships more.

FAMILY

No matter who you are, at the core of your identity is family. You might be from a traditional family, a divorced family, a foster family — it really doesn't matter. What matters is how you honor where you're from; your background, your history and your lineage.

When you look at it this way, instead of judging where you are from, you can open up more of an opportunity for yourself to flourish in life. When you work on honoring your family and doing the small things that you need to do to strengthen it, your life will be enriched, more fulfilled, more joyful, and more alive. Strive to make contact with your family members every week. Check in and communicate.

Support

Families go through turmoil in the form of conflict, disease, death, divorce, and other hardships. During hard times, you have a special opportunity to support each other. Family members can grow closer by weathering hardship. Don't run away. As painful or as difficult as life's situations may seem, you have the chance to foster your family and strengthen the ties that are a big part of who you are.

It is a pleasure being around people who honor family. American tourists particularly enjoy travelling to places where life revolves around family. Italy, for example, where there are businesses and trades that are passed down through the generations, is a very popular destination.

Why does this focus on family interest us?

It is because of the heart-felt energy that is created through honoring family and tradition. Ultimately, it is the bond of love that we admire. Love is what drives our soul to fulfillment.

Communication

Communication skills must be worked on in order to get better over time. If you don't reflect on and practice these skills, they cannot improve. Build your skills by practicing being honest and kind with your words.

Trying to communicate with people who are important to us can be a daunting task. We sometimes hide our emotions for fear of being rejected or hurt. We try to avoid confrontation and drama by speaking little, or not at all. This is a mistake.

As a general rule of thumb, communication should always be very honest, without judgment, and led by a compassionate heart. If you practice these three things, I promise that communication with your loved ones will improve with time.

Respect

It breaks my heart when I hear someone of any age complain about or disrespect their parents. The amount of energy it takes to raise a child from the ground up is not only extraordinary, but it is also such a selfless task. It is a vast commitment, and it is something you're not taught how to do.

So how can we harshly judge our parents when we know, at heart, they truly want the best for their children?

It is easy to point fingers and judge, but how often do we tell our parents or family members how much we love them?

We often let outside factors negatively influence us. Don't let this happen. Keep positive and respectful at all times.

Has your relationship been ideal in the past?

Maybe not. The good news is *you have the power to change.*

Work on the skills necessary to foster, strengthen, and improve the relationship. Does your family stress you out? Perhaps you need to practice some forgiveness and let go.

Family is, ultimately, the wellspring of your life. Honor that by taking time out of your busy schedule to spend time with your family, whether they be near or far. It seems that in this modern world, we have gone backwards in terms of spending time with family.

How many actually sit together as a family and eat dinner at the table?

I think it's quite simple; we just have to make it a priority. Take the time. You may have to plan ahead of time, or maybe use technology like Skype if you are living far apart.

COACHES

What is a coach?

The term once defined a person who embodied mentoring, leadership, support, and strength. A coach was a unifying force that brought everybody together. Somewhere along the line, sports became such a big business that coaches started having to play different roles, more related to marketing and money-making. There are still good coaches out there, but you have to look carefully to find them.

If you have hopes of becoming a great player, you need to be mindful of the types of coaches and the playing situations you choose. Do your research and ask a lot of questions. Be in control of your own destiny and recognize a positive supporter from an egotistical bully.

What should you be looking for in a coach?

There are many different styles of coaching that can be effective, but these things are true of any good coach:

- A good coach supports your growth and the team's growth.

- A good coach is a leader who inspires and brings a team together.

- A good coach is a dedicated teacher and gives you lessons that are customized to help you progress in your sport.

- A good coach recognizes your unique strengths and weaknesses and adapts your training accordingly.

- A good coach always treats you with honor and respect.

Mentoring

A mentor is someone who imparts wisdom. The word suggests purpose, counsel, and loyalty. Also, I think a positive mentor almost always has passion. Mentors don't manipulate or persuade in a conniving way. They are wise and trusted counselors.

In addition to your head coach, your team will usually consist of other coaches, and you may find mentors among them. Be observant in your interactions with them.

Are they going to move you in the direction that you want to go, or are they going to take you backward?

A poor mentor will stand in your way and a good mentor will move you forward.

Be on the lookout for other people in your life who can be good mentors. Think about the people that you keep closest to you right now.

Are they positive influences?

Who are true mentors in your life?

Recognize that the people you surround yourself with will have a great impact on your experience and probably your progress as well. Choose them wisely.

Effectiveness

Is your training program effective?

In an effective system or program, you feel empowered, you find yourself with invigorating energy, a feeling of support, a feeling of love, and a feeling of family. You feel well-mentored and well-coached and have a team comradery so strong that you will feel you could go to war with them until the end of your days.

Great athletes don't need to be preached to because they already have the skills, passion, dexterity, and endurance to be the best at what they do. An effective program will respect your commitment and skills and will foster the growth of the person that you are.

You should never find yourself in a situation where you feel like you are spinning your wheels, losing motivation, and feeling emotionally exhausted at the end of the day. This is the result of an ineffective coaching system.

An effective system will help an athlete become the very best they can be, but will also prepare them with the life skills necessary to become the best version of themselves.

Bullying and Abuse

Somewhere along the line, bullying and abuse in athletics has become acceptable.

Bullying and abuse, physical and psychological, were common practices in both my high school and college institutions. The psychological abuse was varied, ranging from screaming and cursing to derision, belittlement and shaming. Being forced to do windsprints for hours until we were sick, faint, and injured was an example of a kind of physical abuse.

Most often in those days, athletes considered the abuse acceptable. They established no boundaries and were unable to stand up for themselves in any way.

Bullying in any form, be it physical intimidation or emotional abuse, should never, ever, be tolerated.

Do not accept coaching that is abusive. You have a choice. If we remain firm in our commitment maybe someday it will become an unbreakable code among athletes; never accept abuse as a training method.

Carefully choose your coach and your program. I'm not trying to be negative, but thinking as an athlete, if we wish to evolve, break through plateaus, and increase our performance, we have to ask the right questions and be willing to make changes when they are necessary.

My favorite example of a player who was able to do this is the legendary Larry Bird. One of the greatest players of all-time, he chose to leave Coach Bob Knight and Indiana University when it was the NCAA perennial powerhouse program. He transferred to Indiana State in 1975 to play under Head Coach Bill Hodges and became one of the most decorated collegiate players of all time. He later signed a $3.25 million, five-year contract with Coach Bill Fitch and the Celtics in 1979, leading to one of the most prolific careers in NBA history.

If Larry Bird hadn't put the effort into seeking the best situation for himself, can you imagine how different the game of basketball would be now?

Legendary coaches such as John Wooden, Phil Jackson, Larry Brown, and Pat Summit were people who not only attained extraordinary results in their sport, but also set their athletes up for greater success later on in their lives. These players often credit their success to their coaches, and they often maintain a strong and lifelong relationship. I know of such players and I am extremely envious. They would do anything to reacquaint at a get-together with their former coach.

Ask yourself questions about your coach and reflect on the answers:

- What type of individual is this coach?

- What are the principles of their coaching system?

- Is this somebody who is out for my best interests, for the team's best interest, or for their own personal interest?

- What kind of ethics are the coaches applying to their coaching?

- How do I feel about this coach, and why?

These kinds of questions constantly need to be revisited as we grow and circumstances change.

TEAMMATES

Think about the construction of this word: *team* and *mate*. A mate is a companion and a comrade. Because you share so much time together, and share a training regimen that is often intensely difficult, relationships between teammates can be uniquely strong.

When it comes to performing well in a team sport, a teammate is second only to a coach in importance.

Teammates are like supporting beams of a big skyscraper. Rusty or weak beams will be forged by negative relationships that are damaged by jealousy or greed. Stay positive with your teammates and discourage derogatory comments, gossip, and selfish behavior.

Are your teammates encouraging or dividing?

Are they supportive and empowering, or are they constraining?

Positive, supportive teammates promote:

- Achievement
- Equity
- Comradery

These are essential for motivation and ultimately, for success.

Three Cs

The Three Cs in my book are *Complaining, Commiserating,* and *Comparing.* These behaviors are destructive to the cohesiveness of a team and damaging to progress of the individual athlete.

These terms have specific meanings to me:

- Complaining is expressing negative feelings without trying to work out the problem.

- Commiserating is holding complaining sessions with other athletes. Commiseration tends to share and build more negativity; it's amazing how many more complaints you can think of when involved in a commiseration session.

- Comparing is looking at other players and focusing on differences and similarities instead of focusing on your own program and your own strategies for improvement.

The Three Cs are all common negative behaviors. If you see one of them in yourself, address it right away by fighting it with positive thought and action.

They are such a destructive force within a team framework that if you realize someone on your team is exhibiting any of these characteristics, you may want to bring it to their attention, with kindness and compassion, of course. If you have a mentor among the coaches on the team, it may be helpful to point out that you are worried about one of your teammates. The Three Cs can wreck team comradery by creating an overwhelmingly negative environment and that puts everyone's performance at risk.

Ultimately, if it cannot be resolved, an athlete may have to choose to leave the organization. I have found that the most effective way to fight the Three Cs is to lead by example. Be conscious of your words and behavior and stay an unshakable, positive force.

Motivation

Motivation is such a powerful force. People pay enormous amounts of money to go see motivational speakers.

Why is this?

It's the energy behind the words of the motivational speaker that you are actually paying for.

Words are ancient symbols that are expressed through our vocal chords. That is all they are. It is scientifically proven that words create a tone or resonance. Words of positivity create a higher vibration or tone, which make our selves vibrate in response. In essence, this makes us feel more alive, heightens our senses, and makes us feel that we can accomplish anything.

You can see how positivity can lead to a peak performance. The positive vibration is the essence of motivation.

Motivation can come from coaches and teammates, but it can also come from within. A training program lacking motivation combined with a negative attitude can only move you backward and keep you from realizing your gifts.

In contrast, positive vibrations that are directed at training will provide an athlete with the tools or cues to take them where they want to go. Combine that with a self-motivating positive attitude and you will break through plateaus and move up the rungs of the performance ladder.

Collaboration

Collaboration is cooperation. It's working with someone with a common goal or vision to produce or create. In the sports realm, this usually has something to do with striving for a title or championship.

If you are in an individual sport, you are collaborating with your coach, or maybe you have some mentors as well. But for a team sport, collaboration involves yourself, your many teammates and the hierarchy of coaches. You want to make sure you are all on the same page, and that continuity of purpose is never lost.

Ultimately, success in collaboration comes down to communication. It relies on respectful exchanges, shared values, shared vision, and commitment. It can be complex and difficult, but mastering this kind of collaboration is a tremendous life skill, one that will serve you well for the rest of your life.

In any team sport, your teammates should be your life force and your coaches are your back bone. You should grow together and move forward in a way that produces the results that you are looking for.

When teammates and coaches can all work together cooperatively, with dedication, respect and joy, progress as a team is inevitable. Great collaboration leads to championships.

Conclusion

It takes effort, focus, commitment, and sacrifice to gain an edge in an athlete's world. The same can be said for the rest of your life as well.

We hear many stories of top athletes who had the opportunity to shine at the top of their games, but were unprepared for life afterwards. They often seem lost in the post-game world; they make poor decisions, sometimes lose great amounts of money, and their personal lives suffer.

These athletes had the numerous skills required to plan their careers with precision, but they neglected to put the same skills to work in planning for their later years.

Whether you are a new athlete or one at the top of your game, I urge you to ask yourself some questions:

- What do I want out of my life after it is time to retire from the game?

- What do I want to offer to the world that is in alignment with the mission of my heart?

- What do I need to do right now in order to work on my weaknesses and bring more fulfillment to my life?

In your sports training, you will have already identified some weaknesses and have worked hard to improve. It is necessary to look at weaknesses that can impact your progress as an athlete, but can affect you later in life as well. This book can help you identify and address the weaknesses that hold you back from success, happiness, and fulfillment.

This book is merely the first step in a journey. It's a small peek into a big picture. You don't become a professional athlete overnight; you put it together brick by brick. I've given you some key elements to constructing a good foundation on which you can build your career, and the rest of your life.

A good foundation is built by good choices:

- Assembling a healthy team
- Making commitments
- Establishing positive habits

I can tell you that if you work on all the elements presented in this book, you will gain more than increased performance in your sport; you will gain natural life skills. You will discover your natural gifts, learn how to embrace life as an athlete, and learn how to find a new, fulfilling lifestyle after sport.

I'm not suggesting you try to implement every single little thing in this book. Just try one or two per week, and build upon that. Just like in sports, we know there are no shortcuts. Improving takes hard work, day in and day out. Be patient and compassionate with yourself.

Furthermore, I urge you to reach out. If you feel you need a mentor, a guide, and a sense of accountability, feel free to reach out to me. If you would like to work with me, I have an extensive process that will take you to where you want to go.

After reading this book I hope you have learned that you already have most of the answers in your heart. Power comes from connecting to your heart; it is, ultimately about passion and love. The greatest leaders in the world throughout history have known this secret.

Remember to reflect often, ask good questions and listen to yourself. It is my hope that what you have read here will help you get started on a journey that leads to the fulfillment of your goals as an athlete, and will also enable you to take the necessary steps to create the life of your dreams.

Next Steps

How to contact Frederick Entenmann for book signing, speaking engagements, mentoring, podcasts or coaching opportunities:

Phone: (614) 827-5427

Email: fentenma@gmail.com

Website: FrederickEntenmann.com

Blog: FrederickEntenmannblog.com

Facebook: Mind Body Life

Podcast: Mind Body Life on SoundCloud and Itunes

Youtube Channel: Frederick Entenmann

Twitter: Fentenmann

Instagram: FENTENMANN

Skype: frederick.entenmann8

About the Author

A holistic mind-body-life entrepreneur, former Division I and professional basketball player, Frederick Entenmann is a dedicated mentor, guru, and coach for professional and amateur athletes.

With a focus on facilitating both sporting and life goals, Frederick specializes in helping discover innate strengths and assists in planning for a successful post-athletic career. He is known for his rare athletic feats of dunking from the free throw line at fourteen years old, bench pressing 450 pounds, squatting 600 pounds, and deadlifting 690 pounds at age twenty-two; as well as running a sub-four–minute mile at thirty-six years old.

Frederick understands the multiple facets of training organically and naturally through firsthand experiences in implementing and testing himself via his own systems, theories and formulas.

Founding his MIND BODY LIFE brand in 2013, his innovative, organic, and holistic approach helps athletes by:

- Developing stronger goal-setting skills, clarity and focus
- Eliminating distractions
- Conserving and increasing energy
- Facilitating personal growth and expansion
- Developing personal boundaries and leadership
- Magnifying and accepting personal accountability
- Teaching self-love

Specifically, he stands at the threshold of a new era in medicine and healing. Instead of viewing the human body as a biological machine, he teaches how the human body encodes thought, converts it into matter, and stores it as energy within specific areas of the body.

Frederick uses his knowledge of the body as a vast energetic network, where spirit, matter, and power intersect; and decodes the process of how these energy centers work, linking specific injuries and illnesses with past emotional traumas to provide a deeper framework for authentic healing.

Collectively, he holds numerous degrees, certifications, and trainings and is extensively familiar with many studies and practices:

- Sports performance
- Bioenergetics
- Performance psychology
- Rehabilitation
- Yoga
- Meditation

While Frederick has always been physically active in soccer, football, and baseball, it wasn't until he was confronted with post-traumatic stress disorder (PTSD) due to an abusive coaching experience in college that he began this journey into holistic healing. He discovered yoga and meditation in 2009 for the grounding, healing elements that reconnect one with authentic self, enrich self-love, and release traumatic stress.

Life took on a bigger meaning for Frederick as he founded his own life mentoring and coaching practice for athletes in 2014. Through his commitment to his holistic approach, Frederick discovered the authentic benefits of preventative wellness and found that his life mission was to spread positivity and to educate, inspire, and create a healthier collective consciousness. After nearly a decade in the sports performance industry, he now dedicates himself to mentoring professional and amateur athletes, creating podcasts, writing informative blogs, speaking to teams, traveling, being in nature, meditating, cooking organically nourishing meals, and spending as much time as possible with his family, especially his two amazing children, Magnus and Lilian.